AF295367

Haiku 101

For Reading With Some Warm Tea

This is Number One

Arthur R.D. Banks

Omslagsdesign: Dilshan Chamika

Förlag: BoD – Books on Demand, Stockholm, Sverige

Tryck: BoD – Books on Demand, Norderstedt, Tyskland

ISBN: 978-91-7969-079-3

This book contains one hundred and one haiku. It could be read in less than an hour but to get the most out of it read, reflect, pause and ponder, have a cup of tea, talk about it with a friend or why not a stranger. I'm not your mom.

The book took around one hundred and one days to write, so no need to rush, take your time.

The content of this book is just as I said one hundred and one haiku and some art but you can fill it with meaning should you so wish. What they will mean to you I don't know, it is probably different from what it mean to me and that is okay.

Something that hit me halfway through was that some of the haiku can be read from bottom to top as well. So you can regard that as unintentional bonus material.

And in case anyone should ask: The yellow curtains in Haiku 62 are yellow simply because I wanted them to be yellow, it is a nice colour, no other deeper meaning. A little while I thought about making them pink or polka dotted.

– Arthur R.D. Banks

I'd like to dedicate this book to my dear Ellie, death parted us too soon, yet I hope you will enjoy this book with a cup of good tea as intended.

I'd also like to take a moment to thank some of my friends who beta-read this book, gave some feedback and generally brightened some of my days. Linnea, Victoria, Karen, Micaela and Alice, thank you all for your help and great advise.

Last but not least I have to mention my brother who read through the texts, corrected my grammar and found a lot off missing commas. Thank you, I could not have done it without you. – Arthur R.D. Banks

2   13/12-2019

Sun and moon blue sky

Two birds seeing eye to eye

Together they fly

3　14/12-2019

Night, darkest sorrow

Raindrops falling heaven's tears

Will dawn ever come?

4   16/12-2019

A train passes by

Taking people near and far

I want to go home

5   17/12-2019

After work party

Laughing friends, no, family

The happiest place

6

Missed you for so long

Never gonna give you up

You have been rick-rolled

7   18/12-2019

You are my sunshine

Your smile made me so happy

You were my sunshine

8   19/12-2019

My heart is empty

Like the night sky without stars

Now I see the moon

9   20/12-2019

Once close as can be

Separated by sadness

Why can't we be friends?

10   21/12-2019

Strangers on the buss

Living in their own bubbles

Would you let me in?

11   23/12-2019

Small snowy home town

Streets I walked so many times

I really missed you

12　24/12-2019

Dining together

Snow flying in whirling wind

So now it's Christmas

13   25/12-2019

When you're feeling down

Ohana means family

And keep on swimming

14

Feel that weird feeling?

Is the book talking to you?

Yes that is correct

15   31/12-2019

Fire in the sky

Explosions in the dark night

Happy new year folks

16

Rainbow clouds above

Mountains covered in deep snow

Nature's true beauty

17

Find out what you need

Consider the coconut

Trust the universe

18   10/1-2020

Mother and father

Best friends, siblings and true love

The hardest goodbyes

19   11/1-2020

Stand up and let's go

The adventure doesn't wait

Come on it'll be fun

20   16/1-2020

At the final test

How in this world does this work?

I should have studied

21

I think, so I am

Is boredom all I live for?

No, I think not. poof!

22   18/1-2020

Near total silence

Not another being here

Empty library

23

Not just warm leaf juice

Liquid peace and harmony

Tea is so much more

24   26/1-2020

Float little duckling

Over waters deep and cold

Soon you'll fly with me

25

Stare down the abyss

Darkness whispers here I come

Look a butterfly

26

A tree on a hill

Watching the sunset again

The tree was happy

27

Let us flip a coin

Let fate guide our way forward

We'll find our own way

28

A cup my dear friend?

A moment of harmony

Let's drink together

29   2/2-2020

Palindromes are fun

Both one way and the other

Symmetry is nice

30

Fluffy little snout

Fur white as the winter snow

Rabbit friend of mine

31

Waves, heat even feet

All that I see, what will be

My next PDE

32   4/2-2020

Glow little ember

Your warmth is ever welcome

You light up my world

33

I'm not who I am

I'm not "past me" anymore

But then who am I?

34

Is your tea too warm?

Remember that old story?

Good things come in time

35   5/2-2020

So many we meet

And all the moments we share

Adventures of life

36

All are dealt a hand

Life is not fair nor equal

How do you play yours?

37

Sitting in the shade

Listen so the birds singing

My favourite tree

38

Look into my eyes

See my true self looking back

Windows to the soul

39   6/2-2020

Howling at the moon

Echos answering the call

A lone wolf no more

40   7/2-2020

As all things of old

Walk the way of the dodo

All roads go to Rome

41

Flying north to nest

Return home at any prise

Coconuts migrate?

42   8/2-2020

Deep blue eyes of joy

Lost in dreamy starlight's gaze

Not alone with you

43   9/2-2020

Traveling through space?

Prepared for all adventures?

You got your towel

44　11/2-2020

Someone sure loves you

Always remember that, friend

Should call my parents

45

Haven't seen this before

It has always right here

I should explore more

46

This, my self-made cage

What is it that traps me here?

Could I set me free?

47 12/2-2020

Roses in the snow

Looking in to their warm vase

Flowers don't feel cold

48

I may be a book

I may not talk or feel, but

I may be a friend

49   16/2-2020

There's plenty of fish

A sea full actually

But I love this one

50

So much can happen

In seventeen syllables

Life as a haiku

51   17/2-2020

We're halfway there now

Half done, or half still to go?

Now we're half way there

52

Off by one errors

Proof that the small things matter

A programmer's bane

53

Sit on a park bench

Enjoy the world around you

Now take a deep breath

54   18/2-2020

Wind blowing through grass

A moment of inner peace

A walk in the park

55   19/2-2020

Good morning songbird

Singing in the morning sun

Thanks, you made my day

56

The beauty of joy

Sparkling smile of happy eyes

Can I make you smile?

57

Enjoy the small things

Rosy sky, leafs in the wind

Small things cause a smile

58   20/2-2020

Learn something anew

Relive the joy of learning

Learn something each day

59 21/2-2020

I can't believe it

It does not make sense to me

But does it have to?

60

It makes them happy

If it doesn't bother you

Let them be happy

61

Can you hear my voice?

Yes of course, loud and clear, dear

Are you listening?

62

Bright yellow curtain

Framing windows to out here

Let's now see this through

63   22/2-2020

I have just enough

I'm happy and have good friends

I am truly rich

64

Snail in a tunnel

Moving forward slow but sure

Soon it'll see the light

65

Writing a haiku

A puzzle of syllables

A fun little game

66

If I had your eyes

Wonder what wonders I'd see

What do I look like?

67

Late night state of mind

Awake and sharp as ever

Daylight saving time?

68   23/2-2020

Across the table

I wish I could speak to you

If I had the words

69

The world is ablaze

Embers dancing to the sky

I'll get marshmallows

70

To my long lost friend

How have your adventure been?

Call me, I'll answer

71

Problem of rebirth

Let the best of you live on

Yet you have to die

72

Music, feelings true

One with the flowing rhythm

Oh, come dace with me

73   26/2-2020

Empty mind so calm

Nothingness filling the void

Darkness speak to me

74

You're never ready

Trust that it'll work out somehow

Take the leap of faith

75

What scare you the most?

Whatever it is you fear

Learn how to face it

76   27/2-2020

Why is it so hard

To say the words I have to

To open my heart

77

The sun sets again

Just the same as yesterday

Tick tock goes the clock

78   28/2-2020

In darkness despair

The world have left you alone

There must be a light

79   29/2-2020

Start your morning right

The first steps are important

At least make your bed

80 1/3-2020

I can not do it

I would need to work so much

But what if I start

81   2/3-2020

The past gone and done

We all made a few mistakes

Hope you learned from it

82   9/3-2020

I rise once again

Every time when I fall down

I'll get up somehow

83

Cat outside my door

Not a word yet you said all

How nice to meet you

84

It all started here

With that deceptive question

Had to ask, what if?

85

Curiosity

A blessing, a curse, depends

Perspective is key

86

So you want it done

We both know what you should do

Just take the first step

87

I don't have a clue

I don't know a single thing

But I can learn, right?

88

All you really need

A good book, a cup of tea

Friends to share it with

89   10/3-2020

Look upon the wind

Invisible it leaves prints

Can you see it dance?

90

Tree upon the hill

How many sunsets you've seen

Tell me your story

91   **11/3-2020**

The art of nothing

Simple yet it brings me peace

Sometimes that's enough

92

Once upon a dream

I had it all figured out

Gone with the alarm

93   13/3-2020

Content running out

Creativity too low

Let's do the limbo

94

Just one more haiku

I just had an idea

Ops! I wrote a book

95   14/3-2020

Friend, former stranger

Did we meet for a reason

Or coincidence?

96   16/3-2020

Puns are not funny

They're merely weird tiny steeds

Those aren't small horses?

97   18/3-2020

I want chocolate

First I have to complete this

Good motivation

98

What's behind your smile?

Such a happy mystery

Love is in the air

99   19/3-2020

Take a look at this

Every shape of a haiku

What does it tell you?

100   20/3-2020

This was a surprise

I am lost on this new path

Let's see where it goes

101   21/3-2020

This is how it ends

Did you enjoy the ride here?

What will begin next?